Ways into Science

Magnets

Written by Peter Riley

W
FRANKLIN WATTS
LONDON·SYDNEY

First published in 2001 by Franklin Watts
96 Leonard Street, London EC2A 4XD

Franklin Watts Australia
56 O'Riordan Street
Alexandria, NSW 2015

Copyright text © Peter Riley 2001
Copyright images © Franklin Watts 2001

Series editor: Rachel Cooke
Assistant editor: Adrian Cole
Series design: Jason Anscomb
Design: Michael Leaman Design Partnership
Photography: Ray Moller (unless
otherwise credited)

A CIP catalogue record for this book
is available from the British Library

ISBN 0 7496 3956 3

Dewey Classification 538

Printed in Malaysia

Picture credits:
Rex Features p. 15
Thanks to our models:
Jordan Conn, Nicola Freeman, Charley Gibbens,
Alex Jordan, Eddie Lengthorn and Rachael Moodley

Contents

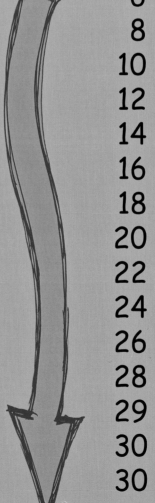

Where is the best place
to find magnets at home?

In the kitchen!
Magnets hold shapes on a fridge door.
And strip magnets inside the fridge's
door help to keep it tightly shut.

The magnets used in science experiments come in lots of different shapes and sizes.

Some are shaped like horseshoes.

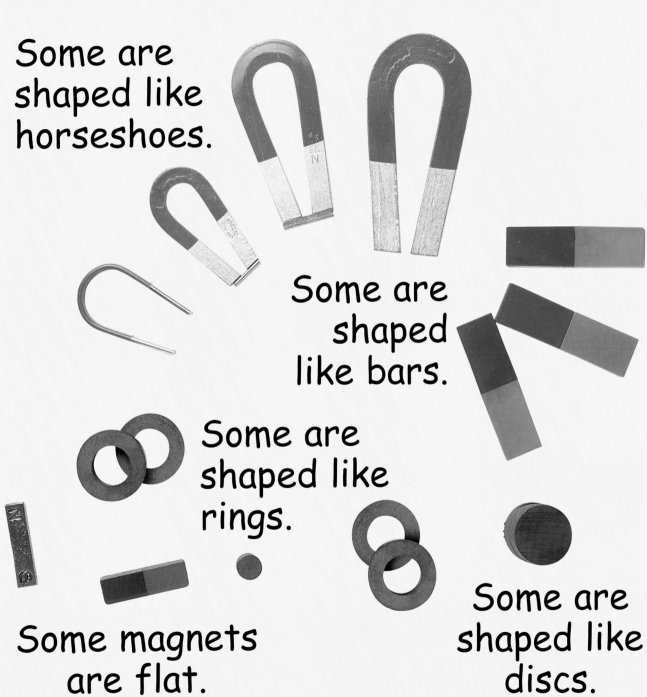

Some are shaped like bars.

Some are shaped like rings.

Some magnets are flat.

Some are shaped like discs.

Sorting  materials

A magnet sticks to steel.

A magnet sticks to iron.

Steel and iron are called magnetic materials because they stick to a magnet.

Magnets do not stick to:

wood

plastic

paper

glass

pottery

Materials that do not stick
to a magnet are called
non-magnetic materials.

Magnetic test

Adam has some objects made of different materials. He wants to find out which of them are magnetic.

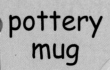
copper scourer

brass door knob

iron pan

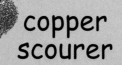
pottery mug

plastic car

aluminium foil

steel bowl

He tests each material with his magnet. He puts the magnet on the material.

The magnet sticks to magnetic materials.

It does not stick to non-magnetic materials.

What will Adam's results be? Turn the page to find out.

The magnet sticks to the steel and iron.

The magnet does not stick to the pottery, plastic, aluminium, brass or copper.

Iron, steel, brass, copper
and aluminium are all metals.

Adam's test shows
that iron and steel
are magnetic.

It shows that brass, copper and
aluminium are non-magnetic.

What does this
tell us about metals?

Magnetic force

Bring a magnet close to a steel spoon.

The magnet pulls the spoon.

This pull is called the magnetic force.

It makes the spoon move and stick to the magnet.

14

To take the spoon away from the magnet you have to pull them apart.

Your pulling force must be stronger than the magnetic force.

Some magnets have a very strong magnetic force. They can lift huge pieces of metal.

What could they be used for?

Magnets have poles

This is a bar magnet. The ends of the magnet are called poles.

At the red end is the south pole.

At the blue end is the north pole.

Both ends attract magnetic materials.

There is a north pole and a south pole on Earth. Where are they?

When two south poles are put
together they push apart.

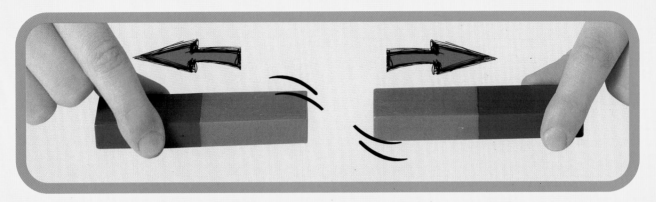

When a south pole and a
north pole are put together
they pull together.

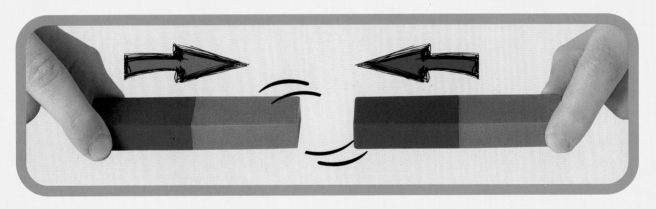

What happens when two north poles
are put together?
Turn the page to find out.

The magnet **swings!**

When two north poles are put together, the magnets push each other away.

Claire ties a magnet on a string.

When it is steady, she brings another magnet close.

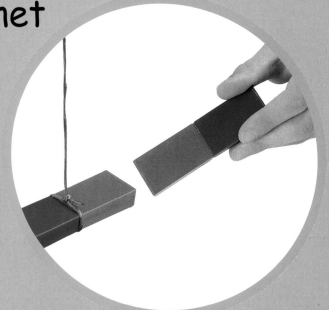

She brings the two south poles together.

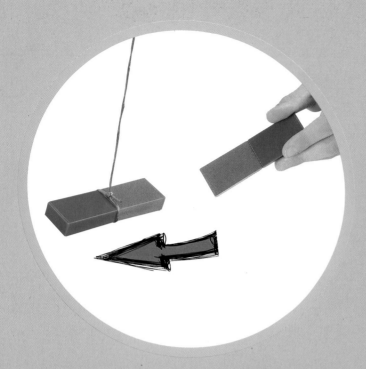

The magnet on the string swings **away** from the magnet Claire is holding.

When Claire brings the north and south poles together the magnet on the string swings **towards** the other magnet.

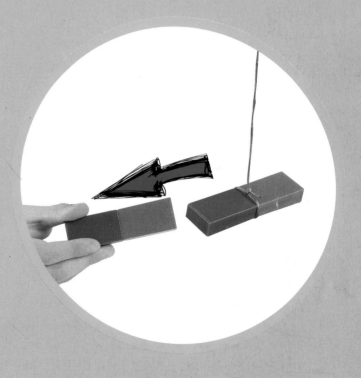

What do you think will happen when she brings the two north poles together?

Horseshoe magnet

This is a horseshoe magnet.

It has a north pole and a south pole. They are not marked with blue or red.

Natasha uses a bar magnet to find which pole is which.

She brings the north pole of the bar magnet to one pole of the horseshoe magnet.

The horseshoe magnet is pushed away. The pole in the horseshoe magnet is a north pole.

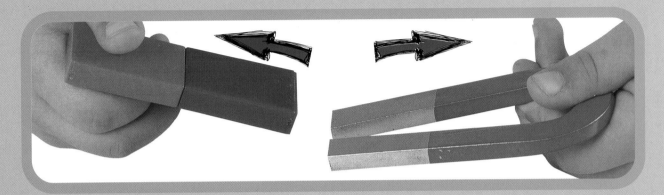

Natasha brings the north pole of the bar magnet to the other pole of the horseshoe magnet.

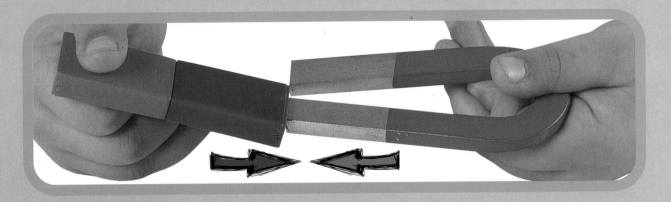

The two magnets stick together. This pole in the horseshoe magnet is a south pole.

Test the 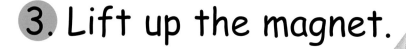 force

1. Test a magnet's force. Put a piece of card over a steel screw.

2. Then put one end of a magnet on the card.

3. Lift up the magnet.

4. The screw is stuck to the magnet. The card is stuck.

5. Now put two pieces of card between the magnet and the screw.

6. The screw still sticks to the magnet through two pieces of card.

7. Try this with three pieces of card. What happens? Turn the page to find out.

Magnetic strength

The screw does not stick to the magnet.

The pieces of card do not stick.

The pieces of card are too thick. The magnetic force is not strong enough to pull through them.

24

Adam surrounds
a bar magnet with
paper clips.

He picks up
the bar magnet.
The paper clips
only stick at
the poles.

The poles are where the magnetic
force is strongest. How would the
paper clips look on a horseshoe magnet?

Which is strongest?

Nadia wanted to see which of her magnets had the strongest magnetic force.

She put a paper clip at the start of a ruler.

She brought a magnet near the paper clip.

She saw the place where the clip
was pulled to the magnet.
She wrote down her results in a table.

Magnet	Distance (mm)
Magnet 1N	28
Magnet 1S	26
Magnet 2N	20
Magnet 2S	20
Magnet 3N	25
Magnet 3S	23
Magnet 4N	15
Magnet 4S	15
Magnet 5N	5
Magnet 5S	5

Try Nadia's test with your magnets.

Useful words

experiment - a fair test.

force - a push or a pull that makes something move, stop moving or change its direction or its shape.

magnet - an object which pulls magnetic materials towards it.

magnetic force - the push or pull caused by a magnet.

magnetic material - a material which sticks to a magnet.

materials - what things are made from, for example: plastic, wood or metal.

metals - a group of materials, including iron and aluminium. Some metals are magnetic.

non-magnetic materials - materials that do not stick to a magnet.

poles – every magnet has two poles: a north pole and a south pole. They are on either end of a magnet. The poles are where the magnetic force is strongest.

Some answers

Here are some answers to the questions we have asked in this book. Don't worry if you had some different answers to ours; you may be right, too. Talk through your answers with other people and see if you can explain why they are right.

page 13 As well as showing us that not all materials are magnetic, Adam's test also tells us that not all metals are magnetic.

page 15 A large magnet like the one in the picture is used in scrapyards to pick up and move metal. Magnets like this can also be used to sort out different types of metal rubbish, such as steel and aluminium drink cans, so that the metals can be recycled.

page 16 The north and south poles on Earth are places at the top and bottom of our planet where it is very cold all year round. The north pole is in the Arctic and the south pole is in the Antarctic. They are called poles because our planet Earth is in fact a giant ball-shaped magnet!

page 19 When Claire brings the two north poles together, the magnet on the string will swing away, just like it did when she brought the two south poles together.

page 25 On a horseshoe magnet, the paper clips would stick thickly around the open end of the horseshoe shape, where the magnet's poles are.

Index

About this book

Ways into Science is designed to encourage children to begin to think about their everyday world in a scientific way, examining cause and effect through close observation, recording their results and discussing what they have seen. Here are some pointers to gain the maximum use from **Magnets**.

• Working through this book will introduce the basic concepts of magnets and also some of the language structures and vocabulary associated with them (for example comparatives such as strong and strongest). This will prepare the child for more formal work later in the school curriculum.

• On pages 11, 17 and 23 children are invited to predict the results of a particular action or test. Ensure you discuss the reason for any answer they give in some depth before turning over the page. In the first two examples there is only one accurate answer, but don't worry if they get it wrong. Discuss the reasons for the answer they give then create other scenarios and get the children to predict the results again.

• You can link the study of magnets into separate areas of science: the exploration of materials and their properties (pages 8–13) or when you look at forces and movement (pages 14–27).

• The simple photographic images in this book can be used as a basis for children to make diagrammatic records of their results in magnetic tests. Encourage them to put directional arrows on these diagrams (as we have done on page 17, for example). This will also prepare them for the idea that a force works in a particular direction.

• If appropriate, the question on page 16 can lead to further discussion of the Earth's magnetic force. To assist in this, the swinging magnet test (pages 18–19) can easily be adapted into exploring a simple compass.